In
Search
of
Home

In
Search
of
Home

S. MONGA

An imprint of
Srishti Publishers & Distributors

Srishti Publishers & Distributors

A unit of AJR Publishing LLP

212A, Peacock Lane

Shahpur Jat, New Delhi – 110 049

editorial@srishtipublishers.com

First published by Launchpad,

an imprint of Srishti Publishers & Distributors in 2025

Printed and bound in India.

Dedicated to Dadi.
A quiet tribute to the stories you carry.

To my mom, dad, and brother—
Thank you for standing beside me, always.

PREFACE

Hi,

I'm Sm.

In Search of Home is now yours, the poems that follow art thine.

Over the course of four prime years of my life, from XVI to XIX, the poems wrote themselves.

They range across a spectrum of topics from Philosophy to Grass, the Clouds to the Moon, and from Love to Loss.

I have used a variety of literary devices and a gentle concoction of colourful, and colourless words, all for one sole purpose—To make you feel.

In a world of blue light and buzzing devices, I'd like to make you go out and listen to how the wind sounds, when it makes its way through fall's amber leaves.

Make you go up to the moony terrace and look how the stars shine for you.

The purpose of this collection is simple. For you to look at the world for what it is. Unjust at times, sour at times, But at all times—Home.

In Search of Home is not the poetry of radicalism. It is what remnants of home slowly slipped out like sand from my heart's

S. Monga | vii

cage over these years. And I want you to have this. It's something very vulnerable.

I could never have chosen to be a poet, the poems chose me and wrote themselves.

And on a separate note, I'd like to thank a certain person or two. Who said to me at a young age, said that Sm you're someone who's capable of things.

I distinctly remember a dear friend saying to me: "Sm you're one of those people who have books published to their name. You're gonna be someone in life. I know."

Here's to you, brother.

I'd also like to thank people who never believed in me. A professor told me at the tender age of 15 that I'd never achieve anything in life. He did this thing where he seemingly predicted the marks of students by looking at their faces. Witchcraft, really.

Foolish witchcraft, though, he said I'd score 27%.

I topped the school that year. And after two years, in a different school, topped all three streams again.

But I reckon there is something in being told that "You can't" that makes one say "I goddamn can".

My father said to me the other day, it is the noise that makes one know that peace exists somewhere out there.

In Search of Home will be noisy at times, scream at you, and stick to your hands like honey and bees. But then, it'll sing to you. It will lull you to sleep. It is the cyclone, and it is its own eye.

"To be a master of metaphor," Aristotle wrote in his poetics, "is the greatest thing by far. It is the one thing that cannot be learnt from others, and it is also a sign of genius."

I've realised metaphor has often been a part of my speech. At times more than I'd admit, I've gone to the lengths of contrasting day-to-day arguments such as a mere quarrel with my mom with concepts akin to nebulas, blackholes, quantum entanglement, escape velocity and red-shift.

Metaphor is a way of thinking and by extension, a way of existing.

Good poetry is poetry of metaphor. Good poetry masquerades itself. In flowers, in the moon, in eyes, in fire, it veils its own self.

All of life is overwhelming at times, consuming even.

If you've ever looked at the world and felt that it's too much, everything is too—Gray... then pick this book up. Make yourself a cup of hot tea, and Breathe.

CONTENTS

SHADOWS AND LIGHT

VEIL

WILTED ROSES

GRAY SPARK

A bird in a distant field, happily chirps
Perhaps the winds whisper, I did smile
On moist days for a split-second, the pain curbs
A gray spark shows itself, then withdraws itself.
Thine bestowed spark I'll not forget, my fellow stranger
What haze is left of it, I'll pick, I'll collect.

NOUGHT

Cold sheets Hot tears.
Warm tea cold breeze.
Chilling darkness enkindling thought.
Hissing temples and freezing nought.
Golden rings ashen fingers.
Love whispers hate lingers.
Soft scent and firm flowers,
Cold Cold are these empty hours.

A TAINTED BEGINNING

I serve witness to the drear end my life entails
For such beginnings never doth entail happy ends.
Never a tree doth bear fruit, one which had been
Poisoned in its tender seedling start.

MASKED POESY

In a gusty loft, I'm sitting
Grieving of wildflowers that fall found-finished
And rose-leaves cursed by a devil's breath
It gushed across my lands and left all that is, brown.
To weep for flowers and greens is poesy
A thing of melody, a longing hazy, a scented glance,
For poetry often masquerades itself as flowers.

DARK HAZE

Are souls made of light? I've seen one
One that reeks of darkness,
Of bitter milkweed and death
A black vacuum of a soul,
A shade darker than all
I tried touching it, and now
My fingers,
are black and blue.
Its poison slowly,
crawls inwards.
The light in my two,
is slowly dying out.
Its mere gaze,
is torturous.
Black haze,
a singularity.
It radiates,
darkness,
wrench,
and empty.
It's overpowering, I
I never could—

THAWED SAFFRON

If only,
Some burn could thaw my numb heart that still aches,
A stranger could hush my ailing neck that still shakes

If my swollen hands wouldn't pain like a thousand needles
And my legs wouldn't creak like ashen-ed dark wood

A meadow of saffron and lilies are bland to my grief-ridden eyes,
Oh, I wish I'd never seen the death that is,
Those two eyes.

BLACK GOLD

A honey of black and not gold,
is what's youth, not old.
A sticky black rush of adrenaline,
Of haste, of musk, of dopamine.
Slowly grappling its sticky fingers onto,
Lusty hearts and pots of naught.
Leaving in each heart, but a little jot.

IN SICKNESS
AND
IN HEALTH

VASE

And one day you come home and find a corpse in the vase
Rosy petals scattered, by the evening ashtray
Day-in and out, you watch it slowly lose its strength
and one day,
The sorrow-wind sweeps its being away
Another one at peace, another life away.

THE WOODS' CONTRAST

High woods, Don't scowl on me—
for my thoughts aren't dark as my suffering,
A thousand blazing stones on my chest but one
Beats of breeze and of peace
Stop these fresh greens' mocking
There need not be contrast to my choking
My Fall, The ashes, My fire, the cease.
A fresh ball of green, and a curling disease.

DAYS GONE

The April sun is all I miss
End of school season, birds chirping
Some sweet song and that concluding class,
Coming home and laying flat on the cold bed,
The pink sheets and rosy pillows
Waking up by grandma's voice spilling
Out my neighbour's secret affairs. Then,
Dozing off again into sweet oblivion.
A morsel of a grown man's heaven

GRIEF

Dead lie the roses, withered lies my heart
O my friendly foe, O here thou art.

My days be soaked with a perverse tart
And moons darker than a witch's heart.

See, when you bailed, I tried to restart
My roses and poems, all fell apart.

So, I took my heart, a shattered part
Crawled through the alley, rolled through the mart.

A lost soul, I met another
A man with a lost brother.

His only friend died a few years back
Some smothering illness, all gray and black.

He looks at hazy stars and sees him
Drinks, weeps and frees him,

From this lonely abyss of a world,
Poor souls' only world.

Old friend, allow me to clasp you close to my chest,
For I have not, a burnt dress and a burnt breast

Allow me the mirage of loyal friends
Akin to heaven, hell and dark fiends.

S. Monga | 13

DEAR STRANGER

Life's candy-crayons have melted,
An unknown sickness ails you, eyes heavy
A knot in your chest, You
Try but you can't breathe
None to make you soup, do
The dishes, Not one who'd say
"Are you doing well, honey?"
Feels dark, feels gray, you feel
Like rotting flowers, Don't you stranger?
Alone in that cage of a room,
Screaming,
but the words don't reach your lips,
I want you to stay strong stranger
Take that pill, do the dishes, put on clean sheets,
Don't look for light in the dark,
Embrace the dark, stranger
Twist the knot till
It hurts so bad, you go numb
And in that numbness,
Find peace, find tatters of love, find hope.

A SOFT BENCH

I've found a piece of my lost-love
A little girl with a basket full of flowers
A fresh smile, glee and fresh-cut flowers
Hopping and falling and gushing like wild wind in the park
In those eyes I've seen joy—That gush, quicker than a lark
A bitter-old book I was reading, on the cold bench
Offered a rose, pulled my cheek. In awe, could a dark heart drench?

AN
UNFORTUNATE
BREADWINNER

To look out the window, to see hope
And watch the sunflowers bloom, to hear raindrops on the
windowsill gush
Look at the day-moon, a green 'scape and squirrels' rush
To be at peace, to be in love,
To sit by the lake, to look at a dove
Hear leaves rattle and snakes' hiss
And sit by a rainy glass and to miss
To feel sun's mellow touch, et feel the moon's bright kiss
is all but a dream—
for a poor slave of bread,
A soul dull as mine.

BROWN SLUSH

A brown slush of fate on a round ball
A picture of grief and a picture of hope on a round ball
Slush in broken-brown huts,

Slush in a golden castle
A raindrop rests on musk,
Another on dead basil

Of hunger and health—a ball of disparity.
A worn-out divide, a divide of hazy clarity.

HOME

BELOVED

Come here now, my dearest beloved,
And leave your boots outside, they seem mudded.
Sit by the fireplace, you must be cold,
Treat yourself with the ones on my shelf, though
be wary of the books old, they're wrapped in dark mold.
I'll put on a kettle of tea and
Look of fresh clothes for you.
A couple towels, a soft blanket,
sweet tangy cookies for you.

We'll talk of poems and hear of scents,
Only you could fathom mine comments.
And gaze at the lost stars like they were once thine,
And find dying sunsets in glasses of wine.
Stay with me ere come day,
of coming in haste, he has an evil way.
Stay with me and look at this pink bouquet,
beloved.

DEAR ONE?

If the trees burned bright and the rills dried up
Will you come back home, dear one?
When the stars turn yellow, and the moon burns out
Leaves lose their green, and to the earth seeds sprout
Honey's not as sweet anymore, the chilis gray
Will you still remember the taste of my tea, or will you walk away?
When a night's all that's left on this world,
All heavenly distance end, Will we have a word?

COLD CITIES

But these cities change who we are, Don't they ayi?
No, they don't deary. One day, when you'll leave
For college, you'll know
You see honey, new cities reflect.
The cities amplify what we already hold,
All that independence,
That raging flame in your chest,
Ambitions
They don't materialize, they're within you from the start
Aching and knotting and bubbling inside your stomach, day-night
So, the city becomes your instrument, becomes the pen to
your rebellion
And you give it the whole of your mind and soul,
March forward like a 'dozer, and grab what was always yours,
The city gives.
But you must stay weary honey,
Don't let the city change you, lest bad things should happen
Dull souls let the city take over them, morph them
Always remember who you are,
Remember what you're made of, dear
Of stars and nebulas,
And honey the stars don't dull, do they?
Oh You've dozed off—Goodnight deary.

A DANCING SQUIRREL

A squirrel lives beside the windowpane,

Often, I see her whipping and whooping there
And wonder if she sees me too.

Her dancing belly swirls in the morning breeze
I hold my quill and drool with no clue

I think she wonders too
If she were a denizen and lived here.
Would she be as pale as you?

DISTANCE

Cooling off on the slab, shriveling inside the hotbox
My mother's roti, the cozy cup of chai, the bread box.

The bottle of wild honey from my birthday trip
My cream old ford, my ancient whip.

The brown ground coffee on my old desk.
My paintbrush, my canvas, once so picturesque.

The little squirrel whom I used to chase through the pots
My roses, my lemons, and daisies with the little dots.

The bag which had some bags and bags of bags
The pencil box my aunt gifted me, the school bags.

The dusty hardcovers, my dusty old bookshelf
My dried roses, the book with the scandalous elf.

I'll swim through this shoreless sea I'm amidst
I'll swim back towards my home one day.

Not wholly sure if it's a place or a way
But my squirrel, I'll come home one day.

WITHIN ME AND WITHIN I

Dilli,
You were prose and never poem like this poem of mine
Within me and within I, we lived in intertwine.
My wants, your alleys. My heart, your pours. My Ghalib,
your gravel.
I've roamed in your veins a decade before I was even deemed able
Mine aching meer and shah-naseer
Thine windy skies thine pink sun byes
Intuitions were never wrong, You're
none but a dreamy song.
I so long for your cold grass bed, lovéd
Cold as a thousand wailing nuns
So, clasp me to your chest
O—Dilli clasp me like you clasped Ghalib's sons.

A HOUSE

Make the bedsheet, and turn the tablecloth,
Dust off the desk and turn on the geyser,
Soak the dishes and check night's spoilt milk,
Put soap in the tray
and steam towels from the clothes-rack,
Ma would you please take care of me
Ma would you please come back?
For I lie by the windowsill and,
I crave my evening snack.

MA

I'm proud that I'm your son ma
Proud of all the ways I've learnt,
You've taught me to keep people close,
And material away
To hold roses right, to
Touch hearts soft.
But Dad's seen the ways of life, the
Ways slowly unravel, ma
Roses and people, they both
Bear thorns, ma
The tree that never stops giving,
Gets burnt to ashes, The candle that
Gives all night, loses its spark, ma
Dad, he seems coarse, seems
Crude, but the world scratched him,
And when he was sore, scratched again
and then again
I get why he looks at people the way he does,
I get why he's always so indifferent, ma
And I guess,
I'm just a young boy stuck in a hotel room,
And I get him because, the world, I
I'm sore, ma

AMIDST GRAY

I'm free amongst the grassland wild,
And yet, I'm lost.
I know,
I know your clouds have found me dilli,
I know this grey old sky,
I know this shushed rain,
And I know this barren lull.
Grey me not yet you sky,
with the same old story,
Just spare me this one bite,
One bite of my flaky sarafa kachori.

SHEHAR

A city of dead saints, Delhi.
A hundred people on the metro. At the exit, a cent more
A craft a day to fill their stomachs; Spite, malice and gore
A place of broken people, a place of broken thieves
A poet's misery and fall's rusty leaves
A blaze and crookery inside hearts' burgundy,
Oh—but I'd heard saints lived here, Oh the death of a city.

ESCAPE

I wonder where this bus leads to,
The barrens of Baskerville which smell of
The dead perhaps, or
A place where heinous giants live, where blood flows in lakes and
mould flows in veins, where death is water and life is sand?
An English cottage perhaps, colored in roses perhaps,
Fields of emeralds and flecks of rubies, some
Place where the days are amber, and nights are ivory
The place of citrus and berries perhaps, the winery?
Take me to the monks' abode, uphill
To peace, and not spite, to lustre, to white.

I see we've reached, o driver
Neither Relief nor a malady?
Oh driver, I recognize this, its—
Home.

SHADOWS
AND
LIGHT

GLOOM

But I cannot attribute this loss to someone else
It was only me who fought and who fell
Not by a thousand blazes and a hundred droughts,
The flower is killed by its own thirst
I can't tell another of my loss, for
Dark is killed not by light but
Its own self-fulfilling prophecy.
It is dark that dwells within I
And loss and grief are but gifts
Of my own black chest.

OLIVE LONGING

Some other tree's been shading the place
Where you used to sit
A wildflower, few weeds, couple amber berries lie,
In the place of your roses,
The forest has no heart, and yet it longs.

PAIN AND YOU AND ME

From sitting merry by the porch to
Shivering in pain, crying and wailing,
Laying in dark trenches in our beds,
We went.
Grandma used to tell me of happy gatherings in their young
Of cheer and love and bells, then
Why is our young lone and gloom
Why does the sun seem darker now?
Why does each soul tremble in pain alone?

PALE DUSK

This cold morning, my blood chills to goosebumps
These old ways feel strangely familiar to a piece of I
This old breeze, this old subway, this old street feels
A rotting corpse of a home to me
The sky slow turns to a yellow reminiscing hue that
makes me recall
pale glow in two cheeks long gone.

RIGHTEOUSNESS

Took the low road home, didn't you young blood?
Resisted, still melted in two arms, didn't you young blood?

Soft lights, Slow songs and Mellow rain is what you were after,
Violent storms were all you got, didn't you young blood?

Tried to enkindle an ice-cold candle, lost your own spark,
Your spark was all you had, didn't you young blood?

Dark skies, black water, not a living soul in sight,
You thought drowning was the answer, didn't you young blood?

A thousand foul stones, couldn't have scratched your castle walls,
You knew not about the rotting insides, didn't you young blood?

Down wounded and bleeding, your last motion was to help them escape,
You expected them to come back for you, didn't you young blood?

A YOUNG GIRL

Am I different, baba?
Why can't I take the bus home like bhai does?
And those long walks around the evening-park?
Why can't I sleep in the cab like he does?
And this pepper-spray you gave me on my 16th
I wanted flowers, baba
A man came to me the other day at the park,
He touched my shoulder, and my knee baba
Was that wrong baba?
Am I a fleshy slush, my bosom and my bottom, baba?
Is my shoulder made to be always looked over?
Why are these people staring?
You see, the other day ma told me,
Her parents never wanted a girl, And
Likewise, you were forlorn when I was born
Is that who I am?
Loathsome, Abhorrent, grim.
The glass half-empty to the brim,
Am I different, baba?

BOILING TAR

My insides are soaked in boiling tar
My poems and work, melting within the blazing black
A strange breeze sweeps low and sweeps far
The whole of mankind, but something's slipped in from the crack
It looks at us, at mankind, as some object to mar
The venom, the animosity—often, I've lost track.

TANGERINE RAINBOW CLOUDS

While I gather berries by the front porch and
Run after peacocks amidst sherbet clouds

A fellow made a dozen stocks and one bagged a thousand
I wouldn't know, I'm chasing a green fox today and

A honeysuckle, a deer and tangerine rainbow clouds.
And mixing cream and milk.

And green and blues and violets
Bluebells, daisies, and cherry vine beds

Well, I wouldn't know.

VEIL

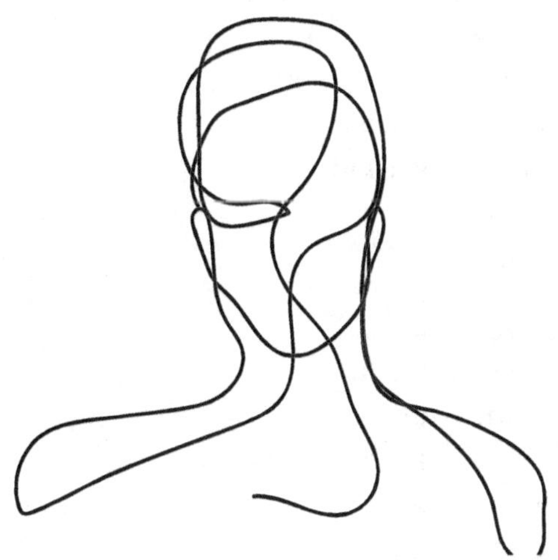

BEE AND THE FLOWER

Whom do you think of – o poet?
Of the one who's forgotten
Or the one you always think of
When you gasp at marble pillars
And castles and flowers and bees.
Now pretend so that the world sees
How much's thine love for bees
While you think of your flower
That the bee doth gently kiss
That the bee doth gently kill
You loved the bee
You loved the flower

Now gone is the flower
And dead is the bee to you
What good's some fruit
When all that was, was the bee to you,
And Gone are the petals
and the dew and the blue
And all that's left is thy blue.

ILL AND LONE

No one to rush in and out,
No wind does gush in and out,
Cold breath in and cold breath out,
Two pills in, two pills back out,
And I think lying under this spout,
Different is sick, when alone,
Family without.

A YOUNG BOY'S DEATH

'twas an evening of smoke drear

'twas the brink of a young boy's wear

'twas a loss of the son, one father's only one

'twas a sun's nightmare, a day to despair, a night so dun

'twas a death uncounted—for the old and young, all one

'twas grief's quite field that spread with no bounds, scoundrels and dusty hounds

'twas a screeching end for the village, a death of white, a death of sweet, a death of sounds.

THE WISE

To carry a thousand boulders and not sigh on one
'tis a rank that the wise run.
When all life's coming to an end,
to be a jack of all, and master of none
Is a rank that the wise run.

To treat failure, like its sister—success,
and practice failure and seldom success
Is a rank that the wise run.

To paint soft, the line between ambition and insanity,
To be a keeper of that grey feather line
Is a rank that the wise run.

NOT A SOUL

Not a soul to gaze upon, not a beat to hear of

Nor a shoulder to hold, and neither laugh to hear of

No dusky skies shadowed above, no birds did cry like this before

Not earth not they not one before, crawled into my mind like this before

Not a hundred but a million stray thoughts, and none go off till a teary dawn

No peace and all noise, none to maybe, soft console?

A RESTAURANT

Chirping under a bright dome, our flock
In a radiant restaurant, we were sitting
French pastries on the breakfast table,
A speck of fruit jam here, a spot of honey there
Rose-tinted sherbet for the others, and
Green apple for the girl in blue
A lifetime of feasting and an eternity of gossips,
Then the waiter came with the bill pouch
Eleven took their pieces out,
One won, giggling
Bid their goodbyes and returning to their abodes,
"30 rupees madam", Did the rickshaw-puller utter
A vice,
A sin he'd done, asking for honest bread and butter
Looked at him with the eyes of a furious hyena,
He dulled, then gazed at the ground,
Reflecting for an eleventh time that day,
"Is it a sin to fill my doll's stomach?"
Flock,
I wonder why the oceans get all the rainfall,
And wildflowers dry and die in the desert.
I wonder, flock
Why is it, that we fill filled voids?

THIS CITY

What good is change and new
In this city of old
Places have stories in their hearts
Of family, of friends, of forbidden gold

ABODE

And now I get it you see,
I never did long for you
Not you, your locks, your love
I only ever longed for home
A feeling.
Something I'd lost along the way.

THOSE DAYS

I'm glad those days are gone,
The grays, the frays,
The dusky days, midnight haze, the giddy gaze
I'm glad old ways are gone

GRAY

Why should I bear this gritty journey, life?
For flowers and moonlight: - I said, for eyes.

But what if I find them devoid, even vile?
Your ma and your pa, look how they smile

Blood may mingle, our thoughts do not, It's a mistake.
Oh the little joys of it: - honey, tea, soft pieces of cake?

All that's gray is life, all which isn't is not.
Grandma's stories, The wizard, the crow and the pot?

Nothing to live for, all ail and all wail, It all's so vile.
A reason to live? Mine's the man in the mirror, the man still alive.